THE GOVERNESS

By Patrick Hamilton

Adapted by
Roy Marsden

SAMUELFRENCH-LONDON.CO.UK
SAMUELFRENCH.COM

ISBN 978-0-573-11158-7

www.samuelfrench-london.co.uk

www.samuelfrench.com

For Amateur Production Enquiries

United Kingdom and World excluding North America
plays@SamuelFrench-London.co.uk
020 7255 4302/01

Each title is subject to availability from Samuel French, depending upon country of performance.

Author's note

On the 30th June 1860 a young boy disappeared from Road Hill, a large country house just outside Trowbridge in Wiltshire. A detective was sent from London by the Home Office to solve the mystery. The child was found with its throat cut and buried in the servant's privy of the house. Detective Whicher, the most prominent of the newly formed detective organisation set up at Scotland Yard, took just a week to conclude that the crime was committed by one of the other children in the family, Constance Kent. However at the subsequent trial the case for the prosecution was found to be unsound and Constance set free. The detective's career was badly damaged by this reversal.

The case was of huge public interest and provided a field day for the newspaper industry. Every week there were new theories proposed as to who had committed the crime, and experts trawled over the house and the archives continually. However five years later, Constance, now living in a religious establishment in Brighton, confessed that she had actually committed the crime, and was sentenced to twenty one years hard labour. She spent most of her sentence at the new Millbank Penitentiary. Although Constance confessed and was found guilty few people actually believed her. To this day there is still debate as to who actually perpetrated the crime. On being released she emigrated to Australia, disappeared from public scrutiny, and died there in 1944 at the age of 100.

Patrick Hamilton must have read Constance's obituary and decided to write a play based on the events. The play was finished in 1945 and was called *Ethel Fry*, a title he later changed to *The Governess*. He placed the events in London, changed the social status, and gave the perpetrator a different motive for the abduction, but kept many of the names and events.

This the second of Patrick Hamilton's plays in which he employs Inspector Rough as his investigator, the character first appearing in *Gaslight*. I suspect that given more time there might have been a longer list of plays and novels which would have included the inspector, and we would have been able to look back with the same fondness we do towards Poirot and Sherlock Holmes. But alas it was not to be.

The role of the Governess in Victorian society is an interesting one. Educated ladies with no marriage prospects and no money had few choices. In 1860 there were approximately 25,000 governesses in Britain and its colonies. They were treated not as servants but then not quite as equals, their function being to educate girls in the subjects of gentility. Languages and social etiquette were high on the list. The sciences of course did not exist, they smacked too much of masculinity and trade.

Roy Marsden February 2015

The play, in two acts, is set in 1860, in the library of a respectable upper-middle-class home in Highgate.

CHARACTERS

MR GEORGE DREW . . . . *a banker and entrepreneur*

MRS WINIFRED DREW . . . . *his wife*

ROBERT DREW . . . . *their son, 22 years old*

ELLEN DREW . . . . *their 12 year old daughter*

ETHEL FRY . . . . *governess*

KATE . . . . *servant*

NURSE

DETECTIVE INSPECTOR ROUGH

RUSH . . . . *under gardener*

JOHNSON . . . . *a detective*

MISS WATSON . . . . *a female detective*

PROLOGUE

The library of GEORGE DREW's house, near Highgate is in darkness. Outside can be heard the insistent drumming of late autumn rain.

The door opens and illuminated by the corridor night light we glimpse a figure wearing a long black cloak and hood, enter. It crosses quickly to the French windows, draws the curtain a little and peers out into the early dawn light.

The figure looks back anxiously before unlatching the window. Immediately the wind outside makes the curtains billow and the window to bang noisily back and forth against its frame.

The figure struggles to contain the disturbance, shuts the window and hurries from the room.

After a short while a second figure appears at the window, opens it and enters the room. It steps gingerly across the floor to the door, and stands listening.

A noise in some other part of the house makes the figure scurry back to the window. But in so doing it bumps into the furniture and the noise of breaking glass can be heard. The figure, ignoring the accident, manages to conceal itself behind the curtain as a shadow appears in the corridor.

The figure in the black cloak reappears, this time carrying a large bundle. The second figure steps forward, carefully takes the bundle, and disappears though the French window.

The cloaked figure secures the window, closes the curtains, crosses the room once more, and leaves.

ACT ONE

It is 8:30am the following morning. Although the curtains are still drawn the library is illuminated by the gas lamps above the fireplace and the oil lamp on the table. We can see that the room is prosperously and profusely furnished, the atmosphere stimulating and cheerful. There are French windows, leading out to a garden with lawn and trees. Against the back wall stands a table containing drinks, glasses etc. Immediately to the right is a tall oil lamp stand with a shade. On the right hand wall is a fireplace, above which on each side, are two gas brackets, each with a round glass globes. To the side is a large desk with a swivel chair in front. Near the desk is a leather armchair. Set slightly to the left is a circular table with three chairs and further left a large settee. A smaller table with two chairs stands against the other wall, which is lined with bookshelves, and into which the main door to the room is set.

ELLEN DREW, *a child of twelve, with a plain, slightly eccentric appearance, is seated at the table in the lamplight, trying to memorise French irregular verbs. She is perhaps too old for her years and has a meditative, precocious air.*

KATE, *a rather plain faced and prim servant, has already lit the fire and swept the grate, and is now picking up the broken glass by the drinks table.*

ELLEN. *Je bous... Nous bouillons, Je bouillais... nous bouillons.*

She looks at the book and corrects herself.

Nous bouillions... nous bwee-ee-ons, nous bwee-ee-ons, nous bwee-ee-ons... *Je bous, nous bouillons...*

She has to look at the book again. **KATE**, *in picking up a small shard accidently cuts her finger.*

KATE. Oh, drat the blooming thing.

She sucks her finger. **ELLEN**, *without looking up, replies.*

ELLEN. You shouldn't say drat.

KATE. What?

ELLEN. You shouldn't say drat. It's swearing.

KATE. Course it's not.

ELLEN. Yes, it is. I know what it means.

KATE. Oh, and what's that?

ELLEN. It's bad. I won't tell you. It's too bad.

KATE. All right. I don't want to know.

ELLEN. I'll tell you if you like.

KATE. I don't want to know, thank you.

ELLEN. It means 'God rot'. When you say 'Drat you' it means 'God rot you'.

KATE. Who told you that?

ELLEN. Never mind who told me. I know.

KATE. You know a lot, don't you?

ELLEN. And when you pull a long nose, do you know what that means?

KATE. What do you mean, a long nose?

ELLEN *extends the fingers of one hand at the tip of her nose.*

ELLEN. Like this.

KATE. What does that mean?

ELLEN. It means go to the devil... And when you do it double...

She extends both hands at the tip of her nose.

... it's worse. It means go to the devil and stay there.

KATE. You think of some funny things, don't you, Miss Ellen?

ELLEN. I think about a lot of things.

KATE. If you didn't think so much maybe you wouldn't sleep walk about at nights.

ELLEN. I don't. I haven't walked about for months.

KATE. Well, I hope you don't. You scare the wits out of us.

The door opens and **MISS FRY** *enters. She carries a sewing bag. A rather beautiful yet disappointed woman, she looks restless, nervous, almost feverish. She stands in the doorway looking from* **KATE** *to* **ELLEN***, and back to* **KATE** *again.*

MISS FRY. Good morning, Ellen, my dear.

She hesitates, and then kisses **ELLEN** *in a rather full and sensuous way.*

ELLEN. Good morning, Miss Fry.

MISS FRY *walks over and sits in the armchair.*

MISS FRY. What are you doing here, Kate?

KATE. I've just lit the fire... I'm going in a moment.

MISS FRY. Weren't you supposed to light it before Miss Ellen began her lessons?

KATE *mumbles.*

KATE. I don't know anything about that.

MISS FRY. What did you say?

KATE *replies innocently.*

KATE. I didn't say anything, Miss Fry. What is it you want to know?

MISS FRY. I said weren't you told to light the fire before Miss Ellen began her lessons?

KATE. I didn't know she was going to get up so early, that's all.

MISS FRY. It's not early. It's broad daylight. Why aren't the curtains drawn?

KATE *glances at her bloody finger.*

KATE. Oh drat!

MISS FRY. What's wrong with your hand?

KATE. I've cut it picking up the broken glass.

MISS FRY. How did you break it?

KATE. I didn't, miss.

MISS FRY. Mrs Drew won't be pleased, Kate. She's warned you before about being clumsy, hasn't she.

KATE. It wasn't me, miss... honest.

She looks aggrieved.

It was broken when I came in.

MISS FRY *gets up and inspects* **KATE***'s finger, takes out her handkerchief and wraps it around the wound.*

MISS FRY. You better get Cook to look at it.

KATE. Yes, miss.

She smiles wanly and goes. **MISS FRY** *walks over to* **ELLEN**, *puts her arm round her, and hugs her.*

Well, how's my lovely, studious girl this morning? And what has she to show her nasty, cruel governess?

ELLEN *laughs.*

ELLEN. I'm all right, thank you, Miss Fry. I've done the exercise and I think I can say the verbs by now.

MISS FRY. Oh, she's done the exercise and she can say the verbs can she? Well, which shall we do first? Look at the exercise, or hear the verbs.

ELLEN. Look at the exercise first. Then I can go on learning the verbs.

MISS FRY. Very well.

She takes the book and walks over to the armchair again.

Not very neatly written out, as usual, I see.

ELLEN. Miss Fry?

MISS FRY. Yes?

ELLEN. Why are you so late at lessons this morning? I thought you were never coming.

MISS FRY. Why was I so late? What has that to do with you, my darling? You speak as though I was the pupil and you the governess.

ELLEN. Oughtn't you to say as though I were the pupil, and you were the governess?

MISS FRY *laughs.*

MISS FRY. Yes, clever clogs, as though I were the pupil and you were the governess. You're very sharp this morning, aren't you?

ELLEN. You taught me. I only asked why you were late because I missed you.

MISS FRY. Why...? Do you love me as much as all that?

ELLEN. Yes, of course I love you. You know I do.

They carry on working.

Did you oversleep?

MISS FRY *doesn't reply.*

I wish I had.

MISS FRY. Do you?

ELLEN. Yes. Because I didn't sleep at all.

MISS FRY. What do you mean, Ellen, you didn't sleep at all?

ELLEN. Rather I did sleep, but I dreamed. I dreamed all night long. It was horrible.

MISS FRY. What did you dream about?

ELLEN. All about baby. It was horrible.

MISS FRY. What about him?

ELLEN. They were doing something to him. I don't know what it was, but they were doing something to him.

MISS FRY *suddenly rises, goes to the mantel shelf and looks at herself in the glass.*

MISS FRY. Who was doing something?

ELLEN. I think it was the gardener.

MISS FRY. The gardener?

ELLEN. He was taking him somewhere. I can't remember. I only know it was horrible.

MISS FRY *smiles again.*

MISS FRY. You're always dreaming about him, aren't you?

ELLEN. I hate him... He's a beast. He tore up my geraniums. He did it on purpose.

MISS FRY. Well, we're not talking about geraniums. We're trying to do our lessons, aren't we?

She returns to the armchair and picks up the exercise book again.

ELLEN. Then when I woke up this morning I looked over at baby's cot, and he wasn't there. It gave me such a fright.

MISS FRY. Oh?

ELLEN. But then I realised that Mummy must have come in the night and taken him to her bed, the way she does.

MISS FRY *laughs.*

MISS FRY. You're a great chatterbox, this morning, aren't you?

ELLEN. I'm sorry, Miss Fry.

ELLEN *looks across at her.*

You didn't sleep much last night, either, did you?

MISS FRY. What makes you think that?

ELLEN. I can always tell. You're all jumpy and nervy when you don't sleep.

MISS FRY. Ellen. Will you get on with your work?

There is a long silence, as **ELLEN** *cons her verbs, and* **MISS FRY** *looks at the exercise book.*

Ellen? How do you spell Parmi?

ELLEN. Parmi? P A R M I...

MISS FRY. Not P A L M I?

ELLEN. No, of course not.

MISS FRY. Then why did you write it?

ELLEN. Did I?

MISS FRY. Yes.

ELLEN. I'm sorry.

MISS FRY. Ellen. Will you look at the exercise?

ELLEN. Yes, Miss Fry.

She picks up the primer.

Where?

MISS FRY. The fourth sentence. *J'ai recontre.*

ELLEN. Yes.

MISS FRY. Read it?

ELLEN. *J'ai recontre le monsieur dont vous m'avez parle?*

MISS FRY. Translate.

ELLEN. I have met the gentleman of whom you have talked to me.

MISS FRY. Exactly. Then why have you written I have met the gentleman who talked to me?

ELLEN. Did I? I'm sorry, Miss Fry.

MISS FRY. Now... the last sentence but one.

ELLEN. Yes. "*J'ai recu...*

MISS FRY. Go on. Read it.

ELLEN. *J'ai recu le portrait que vous m'avez envóye.*

MISS FRY. What does it mean?

ELLEN. I have received the portrait that you have me sent... that you have sent me.

MISS FRY. Then why have you written I have received the portrait that I have sent?

ELLEN. I'm sorry.

MISS FRY. I have received the portrait that I have sent.

She laughs.

Does that make the slightest sense even in English? How would you receive a portrait that you sent?

ELLEN. Well, you might send it to yourself.

MISS FRY. Are you trying to be witty at my expense?

MISS FRY *studies the exercise book again.*

This is outrageous. The last sentence.

ELLEN. *De qui recevez vous ces fleurs.*

MISS FRY. Are you aware of what you have written?

ELLEN. No, Miss Fry. What?

MISS FRY *suddenly flings the exercise book down. It clatters to the floor and* **ELLEN** *scrabbles to retrieve it.*

MISS FRY. You do this on purpose, don't you, Ellen? To vex me.

ELLEN. No, Miss Fry. I don't.

MISS FRY *stands.*

MISS FRY. Well, I shall vex you too?

She mischievously pinches **ELLEN** *'s arm.*

There.

ELLEN *yelps in pain.*

ELLEN. Miss Fry, you promised you wouldn't.

MISS FRY. If you try to vex me, I shall pinch you as much as I like.

ELLEN. You're a savage barbarian...

MISS FRY. What did you call me?

MISS FRY *laughs.*

ELLEN. You're a barbarian.

MISS FRY. What an extraordinary expression.

ELLEN. That's what you are... a savage barbarian, and you are not to pinch me. I shall tell father, and he'll stop you.

MISS FRY. Really? You think so.

ELLEN. Yes. If I showed him what you did to my arm last week he would stop you. It was black and blue, I couldn't sleep for the pain.

MISS FRY. Oh, Ellen, I hardly touched you. It was just in fun, you know it was.

The fun has disappeared from **ELLEN** *'s voice.*

ELLEN. You know I'm not well, that I sleep walk, and yet you still pinch me. You never used to, but now you do it more and more. You like doing it.

MISS FRY *shakes her head.*

MISS FRY. Oh my God...

ELLEN. You used to say you loved me and I loved you. We loved each other. You can't love me if you always pinch me...

She starts to sob.

MISS FRY. Oh my God...

MISS FRY *walks away, holding her head. She leans on the mantle shelf and stares into the fire.*

Stop it, Ellen. Stop that noise, at once.

MISS FRY *becomes conciliatory.*

Come along, my dear. It's no use crying. I'm sorry. I'm sorry. There, do you hear? I've said I'm sorry. I can't say more than that can I?

She strokes **ELLEN***'s hair and her sobbing subsides.*

There now... I'm sorry.

ELLEN. You mustn't do it any more...

MISS FRY. Very well. I'm sorry. Isn't that enough?

ELLEN. Promise?

MISS FRY. Yes... I promise.

ELLEN. Say, Ellen, I promise I'll never pinch you again.

MISS FRY. I promise I'll never pinch you again.

MISS FRY *bends forward and embraces* **ELLEN**, *rocking her gently in her arms.*

ELLEN. Oh. I'm so miserable... I'm ill, Miss Fry. I'm not any better. They said I'd get better. But I don't, I dream all night, and I get so confused. Then when I think you don't love me I want to die.

MISS FRY *comforts her.*

MISS FRY. Sssh... sssh.

ELLEN. You used to say you loved me more than all the rest. And I believed you. I work for you. I try to please you. I try.

MISS FRY. Now then. Don't cry. I've promised you, haven't I? The others will be down in a moment, and you don't want them to find you crying, do you.

She coaxes her.

Come now, smile. Look at me. Smile, now. Look, I'll make you smile. Wait a moment, and I'll make you smile.

ELLEN *looks up at her, trustingly.*

Wait. Look.

MISS FRY *opens her sewing bag and brings out a strange mask.*

I'll make you laugh. Wait.

She puts it on, makes a primitive gesture with her arms, and letting out extraordinary, feral noises.

Ya... ya... wa... la.

She starts to prance about, waving her hands.

Ya... ya... wa... la... sa.

ELLEN *gazes at her, with a frightened smile on her face.*

Ya... ya... wa... la... sa.

MISS FRY *comes to one side of* **ELLEN**, *and puts her face very close to her.*

Ya... Ya... wa... la... sa.

She goes the other side and repeats this.

ELLEN. You're frightening me. You're frightening me.

ELLEN *gets up laughing, and runs away pursued by* **MISS FRY**.

MISS FRY. Ya... ya... wa... la... sa.

The garden door opens, and **ROBERT DREW** *enters. He is a cheerful, flippant young man of about 22, with an amiable nature and a warm heart.* **MISS FRY** *turns and advances towards him.*

Ya... ya... wa... la... sa.

*(***ELLEN** *laughs.)*

ROBERT. What's this then? Is this lessons?

ELLEN. Go on, Miss Fry. Mesmerise him! Mesmerise him.

MISS FRY. Ya... ya... wa... la... sa.

ROBERT. Is this the way you young ladies do lessons?

MISS FRY *snatches the mask off. She smiles at* **ROBERT**.

MISS FRY. No, we've finished. We're just being happy, aren't we, Ellen?

ELLEN. Go on, mesmerise him. Put on the animal magnetism.

MISS FRY. I don't know that I'd be able to.

She smiles innocently at **ROBERT**.

He has too strong a will, I should think.

ROBERT. No, it ain't me that's got the strong will. You must go to the Guv'nor for that. I'm as weak as water.

He stands at the fireplace and lights a small cigar.

ELLEN. There you are. He says he's weak. Mesmerise him, Miss Fry!

ROBERT. She don't have to do that by waving her arms about. She has enough beauty to mesmerise a regiment, just by flashing her eyes on 'em.

MISS FRY. Well, I should like to mesmerise you out of the habit of smoking in the house.

ROBERT. Don't bother about that, Miss Fry. Just mesmerise yourself into thinking I'm doing no such thing, will you?

She turns blushingly away.

ELLEN. Oh, I do wish you would. I'm sure you could.

MISS FRY. Now then, that's enough of that, my dear. It's time you got dressed, ready for breakfast.

She helps **ELLEN** *pack up her books.*

Come along, now, off you go.

ROBERT. And what's my little sister been doing this morning, eh? History, geography... none of Mr Darwin's nonsense, I hope?

He starts to prance around the room like a gorilla.

Ugh... ugh.

ELLEN *giggles.*

ELLEN. No. French. By the way, you didn't hear the verbs, Miss Fry.

MISS FRY. Never mind, we'll do them tomorrow. Off you go.

ELLEN *smiles.*

ELLEN. Do you really think she's beautiful?

ROBERT. Of course I do. Don't you?

ELLEN. Yes, of course.

MISS FRY. Go on, chatterbox. Go and get your breakfast.

ELLEN. Oh... all right.

She goes. **MISS FRY** *sits demurely on the settee, and shakes her head.*

MISS FRY. What a funny child.

ROBERT. Don't know about funny. She's practically dotty.

MISS FRY. It's just her age.

ROBERT *sits at the desk and starts to read his correspondence.*

ROBERT. The whole family's practically dotty if it comes to that. Except for me, and I'm no dashed good at anything... Has the Guv'nor shown himself about the place yet?

MISS FRY. I haven't seen him.

As he reads he is interrupted by someone outside, tapping on the French windows.

ROBERT. Ah, ha. Somebody knocks without.

MISS FRY. Who is it?

ROBERT *laughs.*

ROBERT. I don't know. Come in, whoever you are.

MISS FRY *rises and opens the curtains at the French windows, to reveal* **RUSH** *the gardener, standing there, with a pail and rag. She opens the window.*

MISS FRY. Oh... good morning.

RUSH. Good morning, miss. I was told to clean the windows, if that's all right?

She turns to **ROBERT**.

MISS FRY. May he clean the windows?

ROBERT *replies, without looking up from his correspondence.*

ROBERT. It's not really his job is it?

RUSH *shrugs and peruses the windows.*

RUSH. All that rain last night, miss. It kicked up a lot of mud.

ROBERT. Well, he better do it, if he's got the notion to. Tain't my business.

ROBERT *concentrates on his letters.*

MISS FRY. You may clean the windows, Mr Rush.

RUSH. Thank you, miss.

He smiles at **MISS FRY***, closes the window on himself, and begins to clean it.* **MISS FRY** *returns to the settee. She puts her hand to her forehead, closes her eyes and sits back in a posture of tiredness.*

ROBERT. Exhausted?

MISS FRY. I'm always exhausted.

ROBERT *is concerned only with himself.*

ROBERT. Ah... like me.

The door opens, and the **NURSE** *stands in the doorway. She is an ordinary, shy, capable woman of 35.*

NURSE. I'm sorry, sir. I beg your pardon.

She turns to leave.

ROBERT. That's all right, Nurse. Anything you want?

NURSE. No, sir. I just wondered if Mrs Drew was here.

ROBERT. No. She ain't.

NURSE. Oh, I see. Thank you sir.

The **NURSE** *goes.* **MISS FRY** *rises and goes to the book cases. As she looks at the books she begins to hum the tune that* **ROBERT** *was formerly humming. She starts to sing very gently, her voice curiously compelling.*

MISS FRY. MEET ME BY MOONLIGHT ALONE, AND THEN I WILL TELL YOU A TALE, MEET ME BY MOONLIGHT ALONE,

As she stops singing **ROBERT** *continues the song.*

MISS FRY/ROBERT. AND THEN I WILL TELL YOU A TALE, MUST BE TOLD BY THE MOONLIGHT ALONE, IN THE GROVE AT THE END OF THE VALE. YOU MUST PROMISE TO COME, FOR I SAID I WOULD SHOW THE NIGHT FLOWERS THEIR QUEEN...

Eventually she shyly moves away, picks up a book and sits down on the settee. **ROBERT** *cannot take his eyes off her.*

Are... you going to have breakfast? Oh no, I forgot. You don't, do you?

She shakes her head.

MISS FRY. No... I don't.

ROBERT. Quite right, too. There's nothing so frightful as seeing a lovely woman stuffing her mouth with food. She shouldn't have more than a fairy. Just a flake of honey, and a drop of dew... what?

MISS FRY. You're being very silly this morning, Robert. Perhaps you'll go out in the garden and get me a drop of dew.

ROBERT. It'll be a pleasure. Seriously, though, you ought to eat a bit more. You've got to keep body and soul together, you know. Or perhaps you ain't got a soul, to keep together with a body?

MISS FRY. I'm certain I haven't.

She concentrates on the book.

And sometimes I'm not certain I've got a body either.

ROBERT. Oh yes. I'm certain about that.

He smiles.

And that's a tip top affair. Or am I getting a bit too racy?

MISS FRY. You're getting a great deal too racy. It must be that cigar, going to your head. I wish you'd put it out.

ROBERT. Sorry, Miss Fry. Can't oblige. There's two things I can't resist. One's a cigar and the other's temptation.

MISS FRY. That's very witty. You ought to send it in to *Punch*.

ROBERT. Can't do that. That's where I got it from.

GEORGE DREW *enters. He has an air of supreme confidence in himself and contempt for everyone else.*

Good morning, Guv'nor.

DREW *grunts in acknowledgement.*

DREW. Good morning, Miss Fry.

He has papers in his hand and goes brusquely over to the desk.

Throw that weed on the fire, if you please, my boy.

ROBERT. What?

DREW. Throw that weed on the fire, or clear out of the room. I shan't bother about which.

ROBERT *hesitates, then throws his cigar onto the fire.*

ROBERT. My weed don't seem to be very much in favour this morning. In fact I don't seem to be much in favour at all.

MRS DREW, *a vague, timid, ill looking woman, enters from the garden. She is carrying a bunch of freshly cut flowers.*

Good morning, mother.

She seems curiously distracted.

MRS DREW. Oh good morning... em...

ROBERT. Robert, mother. Your son Robert.

She puts the flowers on the table.

MRS DREW. Yes dear, I know who you are. Did you want something?

ROBERT *shakes his head.*

ROBERT. Me? No mother.

DREW *doesn't look up from his papers.*

DREW. Can you tell me why they haven't brought my tray yet?

MRS DREW. Oh, I'm sorry. Is it time?

DREW *looks at his watch and goes to the bell rope by the door.*

DREW. It's seven and a half minutes past the time, if you want the exact figures. But then I suppose it's no use trying to ring a bell, in a household of this sort?

MRS DREW. What dear?

DREW *raises his voice as if talking to the hard of hearing.*

DREW. I said I suppose it's no good trying to ring a bell in a household of this sort. I am alluding to the miracle of disorganisation such as this household contrives every morning to be.

ROBERT. Oh, come on, Guv'nor...

He laughs.

DREW. Hold your tongue, please. I was speaking to your mother.

MRS DREW. Your tray'll come if you only wait a moment.

ROBERT. Who got out of bed the wrong side this morning?

DREW. If you talk to me like that, before long you won't have a bed, at any rate under this roof, to get either in or out of, the wrong side or the right.

ROBERT. Never mind, Guv'nor. There's other beds, you know.

DREW, *looks at his son, analysing what he's just said. Then, deciding on its innocence he smiles with infinite bitterness.*

DREW. I shall get the tray myself.

He goes.

MRS DREW. Oh dear, why is there always trouble about your father's tray.

ROBERT *laughs.*

ROBERT. You should stand up to him, mother.

MRS FRY. Don't be silly dear.

ROBERT. Well, I stand up to him, don't I? I'm the only one who ever does. Except Miss Fry, and he doesn't ever have a go at her. Does he?

MISS FRY. I think he probably does.

She turns solicitously to **MRS DREW**.

How's your head this morning?

MRS DREW. It's a little better, I think.

MISS FRY. Is there anything I can do?

MRS DREW. No, my dear. You're so considerate.

She presses her hand against her forehead.

There's still such a weight on it, though.

ROBERT. Oh, by the way. Nurse was looking for you, mother.

MRS DREW. Nurse. What did she want?

ROBERT. I don't know.

MRS DREW. I must cut some flowers

ROBERT *shrugs.* **MRS DREW** *moves to the French windows and looks out to the garden, and wanders out.* **ROBERT** *picks up the flowers she has already cut and calls out to her.*

ROBERT. Mother!

He sighs.

I told you we are all dotty in this house.

MISS FRY. That's not very kind Robert.

*(***ROBERT** *stands there looking sheepish.* **DREW** *reappears with a tray on which are coffee and French rolls. He sits down at his desk, and begins to eat. He pours out his coffee, and look at the letters.)*

Oh well, this won't do.

DREW. What won't do, Miss Fry?

MISS FRY. Laying about all the morning. Au revoir, monsieur.

DREW. Au revoir, madame. Or rather mademoiselle.

She gets up and, discreetly gathering the flowers from the table, leaves.

Would you like to look at something good, Bob?

He hands him a paper.

ROBERT. What's this? Is this the Grierson business?

DREW. Yes... or rather a copy of my reply.

ROBERT *studies it.*

ROBERT. My hat, Guv'nor, this is pretty warm. Are you going to send it?

DREW. I've sent it.

ROBERT. And are you going to stand by what you say here?

DREW. Have you ever known me not to.

ROBERT. No. I can't say I have. You're a terror, Guv'nor. You've certainly earned your name I must admit.

DREW. Oh, really. And what's that?

ROBERT. You must know what they call you?

DREW. No?

ROBERT. The Irresistible Force. Have you never heard it?

DREW *laughs.*

DREW. Is that what they call me?

ROBERT. Yes. Didn't you know?

DREW. The Irresistible Force. Really?

ROBERT *nods.*

By God, I'll show that pack of mongrels they are right.

ROBERT. You think they're all dogs in the City, Guv'nor?

DREW. Ninety five per cent of them. And sixty per cent dirty dogs.

ROBERT *snorts.*

ROBERT. You've got pretty decided views, ain't you?

DREW. I've got decided views. Don't know about them being pretty.

DREW *glances out of the French windows to see* **RUSH** *tidying the lawn. He opens the window and shouts.*

Come here you.

He waits while **RUSH** *crosses the garden and enters the room.*

RUSH. Yes sir.

DREW. What the blazes do you think you're doing here?

RUSH. Clearing up after the gale last night sir.

DREW. I'm not talking about that. I'm asking what you are doing on these premises in the first place. Didn't I discharge you a week ago?

RUSH. I didn't think you meant it sir.

DREW. What?

RUSH. Considering it weren't my job in the first place.

DREW. I asked you to do one thing, that was all. One thing. I know it's not strictly your competence but I would still have thought it not beyond the wit of man, even someone like you to take a handful of letters to the post.

RUSH. I did that sir.

DREW. Yes you did... and you posted them without even bothering to check whether they'd been stamped or not.

RUSH. Yes sir... but that be just one mistake sir.

DREW. A mistake.

RUSH. Yes sir.

ROBERT *laughs, earning a disapproving glare from his father.*

DREW. Why didn't you look?

RUSH *shrugs.*

There's a custom in this country to the effect that before a letter goes through the post you put a stamp on it. A regrettable convention you may think, but one which it is dangerous to defy. You have considered yourself superior to that convention, and posted seven letters, at one go, without stamps. That is why I dismissed you and that is why you can collect your monies and leave my service.

RUSH. We all make mistakes, sir.

DREW. So you keep saying. We all make mistakes. But no one makes a mistake of that sort and stays with me.

He dismisses **RUSH** *and returns to his desk.*

RUSH. They'll find you out one of these days.

DREW. *(shouts at the top of his voice)* Just clear out, or I'll kick you out with a stamp on you such as you never saw on any letter?

RUSH *glances across at* **ROBERT**.

RUSH. I'm not the only one that's noticed. The whole house knows.

DREW *gets up and moves, surprisingly swiftly, towards the window.* **RUSH** *beats a hasty retreat.* **ROBERT** *laughs.*

ROBERT. I've never known you not get your way.

DREW. Neither have I.

They laugh together. **DREW** *punches his son playfully on the arm, which leads to momentary horseplay between them.*

Are you trying to flatter your father, by any chance?

ROBERT. No... you've got the spirit all right. I wish I had some of it.

MRS DREW *comes in again carrying more flowers.*

DREW. I wish to God you had... damn you. Sorry for the language, Winifred.

She stands looking out to the garden.

MRS DREW. That's all right, my dear. What's wrong with... what's his name... the gardener?

ROBERT. Rush?

MRS DREW. That's all right, dear. What's wrong with what's his name... the gardener?

ROBERT. Rush

MRS DREW. Yes that's right. As I passed him he was shouting at the top of his voice that "the whole house knows."

DREW. What?

ROBERT. Father's just given him a roasting. We won't see him tomorrow.

MRS DREW. Oh, I see.

She goes to the table and starts to arrange the flowers.

DREW. How's Ellen these days? Do you think she's any better since we cut down her lessons?

MRS DREW. Oh... I think so, dearest. To be honest I don't really know what to think.

ROBERT. She'll be all right.

The **NURSE** *enters.*

NURSE. Good morning, ma'am...

She curtsies.

MRS DREW. Good morning.

NURSE. I'm sorry, ma'am I only wanted baby. It's getting late, isn't it, and he ought to be fed.

MRS DREW. Well... ?

The **NURSE** *stands looking rather bewildered.*

NURSE. I thought he must have cried in the night, and you took him to your room. You often do, don't you, ma'am?

MRS DREW. Do I? Well... I didn't this morning.

NURSE. I'm sorry, ma'am.

The **NURSE** *turns to leave.*

I expect Miss Ellen's got him then.

MRS DREW. Then you'd better go and find her, hadn't you?

NURSE. Yes, ma'am.

She starts to leave.

ROBERT. Half a mo' nurse.

NURSE. Yes sir.

ROBERT. I don't know about Miss Ellen having him. She was at her lessons this morning and she hadn't got him then.

NURSE. Oh hadn't she?

ROBERT. No.

MRS DREW. Well, she must have got him now. You better go and find her, nurse.

NURSE. Yes ma'am.

She leaves.

MRS DREW. Ellen's always dressing up that child, and pushing him around. I shall have to speak to her about it.

She continues arranging the flowers, humming the while.

ROBERT. Well I must be popping off. Are you coming to the office with me, Guv'nor?

DREW. Yes, why not. We can try the new rig. You can drive.

ROBERT. Right you are. So long, mother.

MRS DREW. Bye, my dear.

ROBERT *strolls out.* **DREW** *swivels round and attends to his papers while* **MRS DREW** *continues arranging flowers.*

DREW. What's this?

MRS DREW. What dear?

DREW. This bill from Marchbanks?

He holds it up.

MRS DREW. What about it?

DREW. Who authorised its payment?

MRS DREW. I did. It's for the wood, the logs.

DREW. I know it is. But who said we wanted logs, and who said we were to go to Marchbanks?

MRS DREW. I did, my dear.

DREW. Well, I don't know that we wanted logs, and I'm quite certain we didn't want them from Marchbanks. The man's a blackguard.

MRS DREW. Yes, my dear?

DREW. Have the goodness, not to order goods, or to pay bills without asking me first. That's all.

MRS DREW. Yes, my dear.

The **NURSE** *enters hurriedly.*

NURSE. Can I have a word, ma'am?

MRS DREW. What's the matter?

NURSE. I'd rather have a word with you alone, ma'am, if I may.

DREW. Don't be foolish. Tell your mistress what you have to say.

NURSE. Well, it's only that Miss Ellen hasn't got baby, sir.

MRS DREW. Why should she?

The **NURSE** *stares at her*

NURSE. You said that you thought Miss Ellen was looking after baby.

MRS DREW *sighs.*

MRS DREW. Did I? Oh well, then somebody else must have him.

NURSE. Yes ma'am.

DREW *speaks without looking up from his papers.*

DREW. You say he wasn't in his cot this morning.

NURSE. No, sir, he wasn't there.

The **NURSE** *catches sight of* **MISS FRY** *as she enters.*

Have you seen baby?

MISS FRY *shakes her head.*

MRS DREW. There seems to be some sort of mix up somewhere.

DREW. Nurse, if he wasn't there when you went into him this morning, why didn't you notify us immediately?

ELLEN *appears in the doorway in an excited state.*

ELLEN. Mummy... mummy.

MRS DREW. Be quiet, darling. We're trying to find out where baby is.

ELLEN. Mummy... Mummy, I dreamed about him. I dreamed about him all night long.

MRS DREW. Be quiet.

ELLEN. Then when I woke this morning he wasn't there.

MRS DREW. Stop being hysterical.

DREW. Nurse, what time did you go into the nursery this morning?

NURSE. The usual time, sir. Eight o'clock.

She bursts into tears.

ELLEN. Tell them, Miss Fry. Tell them I dreamed they were doing something to him, and then when I woke he was gone. I told you, Miss Fry, didn't I?

DREW *turns to his daughter.*

DREW. What time was that?

ELLEN. It must have been about five. I dreamed about him all night long, and when I woke he was gone.

DREW. How did you see he was gone if it was dark?

ELLEN. There was the night light.

MRS DREW. Why didn't you tell somebody?

ELLEN. I thought you'd come and taken him.

NURSE. I should say she's dreaming the whole thing, sir.

ELLEN. No I'm not dreaming.

NURSE. Of course she's dreaming. I mean it's so silly. Ain't it ma'am.

DREW *turns to his daughter, and laughs.*

DREW. You'll be suggesting next that he's been spirited away by the fairies.

ELLEN. No... I... I did dream it.

DREW *ignores her.*

DREW. Either someone in this house has taken him and they are playing together, or he's got out of his cot and crawled about.

If he has, he's probably fallen down the stairs and broken his neck by now.

MRS DREW *gasps.*

MRS DREW. Oh George... please don't...

She sits down and reaches for her handkerchief.

DREW. ... but as in that case we'd have found him already, you can rule that out. So all that remains for us to do is to do what it has not struck you to do yet, that is to look for him. What about Kate? Have you asked Kate, or the kitchen staff?

NURSE. Of course, sir, that's it. It's Kate.

Almost bursting with relief.

She's always playing with him and walking him up and down the garden. And I haven't seen her this morning either. That's what it is, ma'am. It's Kate.

DREW *lets out an exasperated sigh, and replies with seeming infinite patience.*

DREW. Very well, Nurse. Go and speak to Kate, will you?

The **NURSE** *goes.* **ELLEN**, *who has sat on the settee, mutters with a strange intensity.*

ELLEN. I dreamed about him. I dreamed about him all night, and when I woke up he was gone. He's gone, I tell you, he's gone.

MISS FRY *sits on the settee with* **ELLEN**, *endeavouring to comfort her.*

MISS FRY. Ellen, please...

ELLEN. But Miss Fry...

MISS FRY *speaks quietly to* **ELLEN**.

MISS FRY. You better go up to your room, dear.

She smiles at her, making light of **ELLEN**'*s fears.*

You can't possibly learn anything in this state. Go.

ELLEN. Yes, Miss Fry. Father. Father.

She leaves.

MRS DREW. Oh dear, that child is a problem, isn't she? She quite upset me for a moment.

MISS FRY *smiles sympathetically.*

MISS FRY. Yes... but she's only a child. One needs to be gentle but firm.

DREW *nods paternally at* **MISS FRY**.

DREW. Yes, my dear. You did quite right.

MRS DREW. You don't think baby could have got out of his cot, do you.

DREW. It may have escaped your notice, Winifred, but our child has only just learned to crawl, let alone walk, so the likelihood of...

MRS DREW. Oh, George...!

She is on the verge of tears again. **MISS FRY** *takes her hand.*

MISS FRY. Ellen's upset you, that's all.

MRS DREW. You don't think he could have got into a cupboard or anything, do you? Or fallen down anything, could he?

DREW. Winifred... !!

MRS DREW. I'm sorry, my dear. But it is a little worrying.

DREW *shakes his head.*

DREW. Well, go and help look then.

MRS DREW, *admonished by her husband, gets up.*

MISS FRY. Would you like me to come with you?

MRS DREW. No, my dear, I'll find him.

She smiles wearily.

It's puzzling, isn't it? Why should Kate take him?

She leaves. **DREW** *concentrates on his business at the desk while* **MISS FRY** *returns to her book.*

DREW. A certain amount of excitement in the household this morning, I believe, Miss Fry.

MISS FRY. A certain amount, Mr Drew.

DREW. But then, women are excitable creatures, are they not, Miss Fry?

MISS FRY. Very excitable... at times.

They work in silence for a short time. Eventually **MISS FRY** *puts her book down and gets up.*

Isn't it time you went and counted your millions in the city?

DREW *looks at his watch.*

DREW. Why, yes. I believe it is.

He collects his papers.

I believe it is. Very well, then. I shall go and count my millions.

There is a strange atmosphere between them.

MISS FRY. Mind you count them well.

DREW. As well as I can, Miss Fry.

MISS FRY. I know a way to make you count them better.

MISS FRY *moves closer to him.*

DREW. Do you, Miss Fry? What's that?

MISS FRY. At least I think I know a way to make you count them better.

DREW. Really? I really wish you would tell me how,

She suddenly advances on him and kisses him in the most lascivious way. He takes her in his arms, eagerly kissing her back.

MISS FRY. Will that make you count them better, Mr Drew?

She kisses him again.

DREW. Now... now, that's enough. I'm not the man I was last night.

She smiles meltingly at him.

MISS FRY. I should hope not.

She laughs. **DREW** *glances at himself in the mantel mirror, adjusting his neck linen. He whispers.*

DREW. Till tonight.

MISS FRY. Very well... till tonight again.

She smiles.

Now go and count your millions, you odious monster.

She sits down on the settee. He crosses to her and she stares up at him in a meekly submissive manner.

DREW. That look is worth everything.

MISS FRY. I wonder. Go on, go and count your millions.

DREW *playfully adopts a masterful tone.*

DREW. Yes. Yes well, Miss Fry. I must be off. I trust my young son comes to light.

She picks up her book again.

MISS FRY. Yes. I trust so. Good morning, Mr Drew.

DREW. Good morning, Miss Fry,

He bows and leaves. Left alone **MISS FRY** *sits and listens. There are faint cries in the distance of* **MRS DREW**. *"***NURSE***…* **NURSE***. Where are you* **NURSE***". She gets up, listens at the door, rummages in her bag and produces a mirror. She looks at herself and, hastily taking a little pot out of her handbag, applies rouge to her face. There is a knock at the door and she quickly puts the pot away.*

MISS FRY. Come in.

KATE *enters.*

Yes. What do you want, Kate?

KATE. I only wanted the tray if the master's finished with it.

MISS FRY. Very well. There it is.

KATE *comes forward to collect the tray as the* **NURSE** *passes the open door.*

NURSE. Oh, there you are.

She enters the room.

You've got baby, ain't you? You've been playing with him?

KATE *shakes her head.*

KATE. I ain't.

NURSE. Put that tray down

KATE *is rather startled by her tone.*

KATE. Who you talking to?

NURSE. This ain't a lark.

KATE. What's all this about?

NURSE. Haven't you got baby?

KATE. Course not. He ain't my pigeon, is he? Wot you goin' on about?

NURSE. He's gone! He was took from his cot this morning and e's gone, that's all.

KATE *looks from* **NURSE** *to* **MISS FRY** *and back again.*

KATE. And you think it's me that's done it?

MRS DREW *and* **ELLEN** *enter.*

MISS FRY. Kate, stop it!

KATE. Well… she's trying to blame me, ain't she?

NURSE. We've got to find him before 'is mother knows.

MISS FRY. His mother's here, Nurse.

The **NURSE** *whirls round to see* **MRS DREW**.

NURSE. Ma'am...

MRS DREW. If baby's gone we must look for him, mustn't we? That's what we all must do. We must look for him. Has the master left yet?

KATE. No ma'am, he's gone to the stables.

NURSE. It'll be all right, ma'am. It'll be all right.

MRS DREW *sees* **RUSH** *in the garden, goes to the French windows and calls for him.*

MRS DREW. Mr Rush... Mr Rush... come here. Quickly.

MISS FRY. Don't vex yourself my dear. There's bound to be a logical explanation.

RUSH *comes to the French windows.*

RUSH. Did you want me ma'am?

MRS DREW. Yes... Run to the stables, will you. Stop my husband leaving.

RUSH. Yes ma'am.

He turns to leave.

MRS DREW. It seems we can't find baby.

RUSH. When was he last seen?

MRS DREW. This morning, early this morning. He wasn't in his cot.

RUSH. Right, ma'am. I'll get the governor. You must organise a search.

KATE. What's the use of searching? It's the gypsies...

MRS DREW. Don't be silly, dear.

KATE. It's them gypsies, that's what it is. They've been hanging around here. I've seen them.

RUSH *speaks firmly to* **KATE**.

RUSH. Kate go and tell Cook, and then search upstairs. Nurse check the master bedrooms.

KATE *and the* **NURSE** *leave. He turns to* **MISS FRY**.

I suggest Miss Fry, that you stay here and keep Mrs Drew company.

MRS DREW. Can't I help?

RUSH. There's no need, ma'am.

As he turns to leave **ELLEN** *points at him.*

ELLEN. You took him. I dream't it. You took him. You were doing something with him.

RUSH *glances at* **ELLEN**, *shakes his head and hurries off to the stables.*

MISS FRY. Ellen, I think it best if you went to your room.

ELLEN. But Miss Fry.

MISS FRY. At once, Ellen.

ELLEN. Yes, Miss Fry.

ELLEN *leaves.* **MISS FRY** *takes* **MRS DREW***'s arm and guides her towards the settee.*

MRS DREW. You don't think it could be the gypsies, do you?

MISS FRY. Come along, dear. It's all a misunderstanding that's all. There's no need to fret, they'll find him tucked up somewhere.

MRS DREW. Do you think perhaps he's in the garden. He might have gone down the steps...

MISS FRY. They'll search. If he's out there they'll find him.

MRS DREW. He might be in some cupboard somewhere?

MISS FRY. Yes. But they'll look.

MRS DREW. What did Ellen mean when she said that the gardener had taken him?

MISS FRY *shakes her head.*

MISS FRY. Oh, that's just Ellen.

MRS DREW. What shall we do?

Footsteps can be heard running along corridors, voices calling out for baby. **RUSH** *is seen hurrying across the garden.*

Oh, dear, help me, please...

MISS FRY. Look at me... look at me.

MRS DREW. I'm frightened... I'm so frightened.

MISS FRY. There... there.

MRS DREW *looks up and notices* **ROBERT**, *looking dishevelled, who has rushed into the room.*

ROBERT. Mother...

MRS DREW. Where's your father? Why aren't you searching?

He just stands there.

There's something the matter, isn't there?

ROBERT. Now then mother. You've got to stand up to it. I've searched everywhere.

MRS DREW. What do you mean you've searched.

ROBERT. The whole place high and low.

MRS DREW. You can't have done.

ROBERT. Steady mother.

DREW *hurries in from the garden.*

DREW. We've searched every room, top and bottom, in and out. Baby ain't in the house.

DREW *turns to* **RUSH** *who has appeared in the doorway.*

Have you searched the cellars?

RUSH. Yes, sir.

DREW. Then try the attic.

ROBERT. I've looked, guv'nor.

DREW *shouts at* **RUSH**.

DREW. Then look again.

RUSH *hurries away.*

MRS DREW. The garden. He must be in the garden.

ROBERT. No, he ain't in the garden. I've looked. He ain't about. He's been taken.

MRS DREW *cries out.*

MRS DREW. What are we to do? What are we going to do?

DREW *puts his hand on her shoulder.*

DREW. Quiet dear. We're still looking. Bob, run and fetch the police. Hurry... there's no time to waste..

As **ROBERT** *reaches the door* **DREW** *stops him.*

And Bob... be discreet.

ROBERT. Yes, guv'nor.

He runs out. **DREW** *is visibly shaken by events.*

DREW. I... I better check the hot houses again.

He hurries out into the garden. **MISS FRY** *turns to comfort* **MRS DREW**.

MRS DREW. Who should want my baby? What could they do with him? He's mine.

MISS FRY *puts her arms around her.*

MISS FRY. Quiet now. Quiet.

MRS DREW. Miss Fry. They've got my baby. They've got my little baby. My little baby boy.

MISS FRY. Quiet, my dear.

MISS FRY *takes her in her arms.*

MRS DREW. God give me back my baby. God give me back my baby. God give me back my baby.

MISS FRY *gently rocks her to and fro.*

Who should want him? Who should want my baby?

She breaks down completely.

Who should want my baby?

MISS FRY. It's all right. It's all right.

Somewhere in the house the plaintiff calls for baby can still be heard as the lights dip to blackout. As they come on again it is evening time six months later. The oil lamps and the gas globes above the mantel shelf are lit and there is a cosy indolent atmosphere about the room. **MISS FRY** *is sitting on the settee, with a book open in front of her.* **ELLEN** *is at the table, still thumping her forehead, as she repeats out loud a passage from Milton's Il Penseroso.*

ELLEN. "I remember, I remember

The roses, red and white,

The violets and the lily cups,

Those flowers made of light.

The lilacs where the robin built,

And where my brother set

The Laburnum on his birthday..."

She starts to cry.

MISS FRY. Ellen. Don't you think it's time you got baby off your mind.

ELLEN. I still don't believe he's dead.

I remember, I remember

The house where I was born,

The little window where the sun
Came peeping in at morn
He never came a wink too soon.
I've just remembered something. I
must have been sleep walking that night.

MISS FRY. How do you know?

ELLEN. You know the scent you use.

MISS FRY. Yes

ELLEN. That morning... The morning baby was taken I woke up smelling of it.

MISS FRY. Really

ELLEN. So I must have been in your room that night, but then if I was why didn't I wake you up? You must have been there.

MISS FRY. Collect your books and off to bed.

ELLEN. Yes Miss Fry.

She goes to the table to collect her books. **MISS FRY** *glances at herself in the mantel mirror.*

Is it true that you secretly paint?

MISS FRY. What do you mean?

ELLEN. Down in the kitchen they say you paint.

MISS FRY *is immediately on her guard.*

I know you don't paint watercolours, so I suppose they must mean you paint your face.

MISS FRY. Really. What an extraordinary idea.

She laughs.

Do you imagine I do that?

ELLEN. Oh, no. You're too beautiful to have to paint.

MISS FRY. I wouldn't go about repeating things like that, if I were you.

ELLEN. I'm sorry. There I go again, chatterbox, chatterbox...

DREW *enters.*

DREW. What are you chattering about, now?

MISS FRY *smiles.*

MISS FRY. Oh, nothing. We were talking about painting. About painting watercolours weren't we, Ellen?

ELLEN. Yes, father.

He looks at his watch.

DREW. You should be in bed, young lady. What are you doing studying at this time of night?

ELLEN. It's mother's idea.

MISS FRY. She thought it might help Ellen sleep better.

He grunts in disbelief.

ELLEN. Good night, father.

She kisses him.

Good night, Miss Fry.

ELLEN *runs over and kisses her.*

Good night father. And God bring baby back.

She goes. **MISS FRY** *stares at him as he returns to his desk. He does not respond. She gathers her things and leaves.* **KATE** *enters and curtsies.*

KATE. Excuse me, sir. There's a gentlemen to see you.

DREW. At this time of night.

He looks at his watch.

What's his name?

KATE. His card, sir.

She proffers the salver. **DREW** *takes the card and looks at it.*

DREW. Tell the gentleman I'm not at home,

KATE. Yes, sir.

She goes. He studies the calling card, turns it over and looks at its back. There is a knock and **KATE** *opens the door again.*

Please, sir, I'm sorry, sir.

DREW. Yes, Kate.

KATE. He says you are at home, sir, because he saw you come in. And he says you couldn't say you weren't at home unless you were, sir. I'm sorry, sir.

DREW. He said that?

KATE. Yes, sir.

DREW. Just tell him I'm busy.

KATE. Yes, sir.

She goes. **DREW** *starts to deal with his correspondence.* **KATE** *reappears.*

I'm sorry, sir.

DREW. Well, what is it?

KATE. He says so is he.

DREW. So is he what?

DETECTIVE INSPECTOR ROUGH *enters the open doorway. He has obviously followed* **KATE** *up the stairs. He is well over 50, greying, wiry, active, brusque, overbearing. He has a preoccupied expression, and looks at the floor.* **KATE** *hovers in the doorway.*

ROUGH. Busy, sir. Extremely busy.

He turns to **KATE**.

Thank you, Kate. You can go.

KATE. Thank you sir.

KATE *curtsies and hurries out, closing the door behind her. This uninvited invasion catches* **DREW** *on the raw.*

DREW. Who the blazes are you giving orders to.

ROUGH. I'm very pleased to meet you, Mr Drew.

DREW *ignores him, and walks over to tidy a book left on the settee.*

DREW. Then it takes damned little to please you, sir, that's all I can say. Moreover your pleasure is likely to be extremely brief, because I'm going to kick you out.

ROUGH. Oh yes...

DREW. Yes!

ROUGH. You said yes?

DREW. Yes, I did.

ROUGH. Yes... I can see you are the sort of man the world says you are.

DREW. Oh, and what sort of man is that?

ROUGH. You have a reputation I believe, in the City.

DREW *puts the book in the bookcase.*

DREW. Do you know what they call me in the City?

ROUGH. No I don't. But you obviously want to tell me.

DREW. I am called the Irresistible Force,

ROUGH. I see.

He rolls the word around his mouth.)

The Irresistible Force. How remarkable. Do you know what I'm called in my job, Mr Drew?

DREW. No... what are you called?

ROUGH. The Irremovable object. Isn't that wonderful.

DREW. Why so?

ROUGH. It's a mystery... it's a miracle. It might be the clue to the universe. The Irresistible Force meets the Irremovable Object. What happens? We should call in a body of scientific men to observe us.

DREW. Are you going to clear out of my house?

ROUGH *takes off his coat and scarf.*

Detective Inspector Rough. Great Scotland Yard. You have a great air about you, a very great air of insolence. But you're going to find, before you've been very long with me that I'm not such a fool...

ROUGH. ... as you look. No I quite agree with you.

DREW. What do you mean you quite agree with me.

ROUGH. I quite agree with you that you are not such a fool as you look.

DREW. Are you calling me a fool, sir?

ROUGH. No. You are.

DREW *is irritated, but wrong footed, by* **ROUGH***'s manner.*

DREW. Is there any reason why I should not throw you out?

ROUGH. No. None whatsoever.

DREW. You seem to think that because you are a policeman you cannot be thrown out.

ROUGH. Yes, That is true. Policemen do not control me. I control policemen.

ROUGH *wanders over and peruses the bookshelves.*

Something has struck me, Mr Drew.

DREW. What's that?

ROUGH. Why, that drink is a friendly thing. A reconciler, sir. A sort of irresistible force itself, between two men inclined to be well disposed.

DREW. Are you asking for a drink?

ROUGH. I am not going out of my way not to ask you for one.

DREW *ignores this implied request.*

DREW. What's your business here?

ROUGH. Why, sir, you must have guessed, surely. It's your business after all, very much more than mine.

DREW. My business more than yours. How so?

ROUGH. It's my business merely as a policeman but it's yours as a father.

DREW. Oh, I see, so that's what this is about. You've come about my son... after all this time?

ROUGH. What does time matter? What should the passage of time matter to a father, in a case of this sort?

DREW. That matter is done with. The matter is closed. Listen Inspector... my child has gone, taken from this house six months ago. To me he is as dead as though he died of the croup or of the cholera. Children die that way, in their thousands and hundreds of thousands. Mine was one of them. The matter must be closed, shut up. I have no hope of seeing my son again, and I have no desire.

ROUGH. By which you mean that you have strangled all hope and all desire.

DREW. Have it whichever way you like, sir. My child was taken off by the croup or by the cholera.

ROUGH. No he wasn't. He was taken off by another bacillus. Bacillus homo sapiens, a dirtier and darker and more dangerous bacillus, I sometimes think, than all the others put together. I'm a student of that bacillus, sir, and of the ways in which it works. I have a feeling that this case is by no means closed.

DREW. It is to me, Inspector.

END OF ACT ONE

ACT TWO

DREW *is standing by the fireplace.*

DREW. I was a trifle off hand with you when you came in just now. I apologise.

ROUGH. Off hand? Yes. A little.

DREW. Or damned rude, if you like, but I'll tell you why. Because you come from the police force, and I loathe the whole body of you. Since my son's disappearance six months ago I have suffered more from your body of men, sir, than I have suffered from anything in my whole life. They came in here, a bunch of loud mouthed, flat footed, incompetents, who went trampling over my house, pulling things to pieces, poking here and there, questioning all and sundry, ruining the health and sleep of everyone in my household, eating and drinking in my kitchen, blabbing off their mouths to the newspapers, calling the attention of the whole of England to our personal tragedy, and with what result, sir? The result that they found nothing. My child has gone, sir. Whether it was a local murdering maniac, or whether it was a personal enemy of mine, no one will ever know. But I want no help from the police in my surmise.

ROUGH. I agree about the constabulary, sir. But I represent a special body of men under the jurisdiction of the Home Office and I can assure you that we will treat you and your family with much greater discretion.

ROUGH *stares at* **DREW.**

DREW. Six months ago life was happy and harmonious. Now my wife spends most of her time in bed, my eldest son seeks solace in drink and I have little appetite for work or indeed for pleasure. My life has become sour.

ROUGH *inspects the bookcases.*

ROUGH. I have a suspicion that you're not a bad man.

DREW. What do you mean by that?

ROUGH. Nothing more than what I say.

DREW. Well... I am much obliged for your compliment. A somewhat small sized one if I may say so.

ROUGH. It's only a small sized suspicion.

DREW. You talk in riddles, Inspector,

ROUGH. Never mind. We shall solve everything before we're done. What about my drink?

DREW. You'd like one?

ROUGH. Naturally.

DREW. What do you want?

ROUGH. Whisky will do.

DREW *crosses to the drinks table.*

DREW. Is there some specific reason you calling here today? Have you discovered new evidence.

ROUGH *shakes his head.*

ROUGH. Unfortunately not. No new evidence, exactly, or rather no exact new evidence. You see evidence is a thing which...

The door opens and **MISS FRY** *enters.*

MISS FRY. Oh, I'm sorry.

DREW. Miss Fry. Come in.

MISS FRY. I'm sorry... I'm interrupting. I only came for my book. I left it on the sofa, I think.

DREW. That's all right. Come in and get it.

She goes to the settee.

MISS FRY. That's funny. It was here.

ROUGH. I remember you putting it on the bookshelf.

She looks at **DREW** *rather nervously.*

DREW. Did I?

ROUGH. Yes. You put it on the shelf,

MISS FRY. Aren't you going to introduce me?

DREW. Oh... I'm sorry. I'm very sorry. This is a friend of mine. This is... a... Mr Rogers. Mr Rogers is a business associate, Miss Fry.

MISS FRY. Good evening.

ROUGH. Good evening Miss Fry,

They shake hands.

DREW. Miss Fry's my governess.

ROUGH. Your governess? That surprises me. I didn't know anyone could govern you.

MISS FRY. I think you mean your children's governess, Mr Drew.

DREW. No. Yes. I should have said my daughter's governess.

DREW *is embarrassed.*

Well, where is this book?

MISS FRY. I'll look.

MISS FRY *goes to the bookshelves.*

Don't bother, sir, I'll find it.

ROUGH. What is it called?

MISS FRY. Oh... it's only a silly book. I wouldn't like to tell you its name.

She turns to **ROUGH.**

Don't you bother, I'll find it.

ROUGH. Mr Drew put it slantways along the top.

MISS FRY. Ah, yes, here it is.

She fishes it out and turns to leave.

I'm so sorry to have troubled you. Goodbye, Mr. Rogers.

ROUGH. Oh, I'm sure it's not goodbye. Au revoir Miss Fry.

MISS FRY *hesitates for a fraction of a second.*

MISS FRY. Au revoir...

She goes.

DREW. Well, now... what was I doing?

ROUGH. Getting me a drink.

DREW. Ah yes. A drink before you go.

ROUGH. No... just a drink, Mr Drew.

DREW. We shall see, Mr Irremovable Object.

ROUGH. Yes, we shall, Mr Irresistible Force.

They laugh. **DREW** *goes back to the drinks table and pours a whisky. He adds soda water and hands it to* **ROUGH.**

Thank you. A very handsome woman, Miss Fry.

DREW. You think her handsome?

ROUGH. Unless you put a magnifying glass on her. I would say she painted, wouldn't you?

DREW *shrugs*

DREW. How should I know?

ROUGH. I should have thought you would have known.

DREW. Would you? Why?

ROUGH. I should have thought so. But then perhaps you don't know a great deal about women.

DREW. No. I know very little about women.

ROUGH. There you differ from me. I make it a point to know more about women than I know about men.

He takes a swig of his whisky.

Talking about women has it ever occurred to you, I mean in relation to your recent tragedy...?

DREW. What?

ROUGH. Has it never occurred to you that it might be a woman after all?

DREW. A woman? How?

ROUGH. A woman, right at the heart of it.

DREW. You mean a gypsy... or a...

ROUGH. No, sir. Quite another sort of woman.

ROUGH *stares at him.*

You originally stated that on the night your son was taken you distinctly remember checking the security of the house.

DREW. There was a storm that night and before I retired I double checked all the locks and bolts.

ROUGH. The police found nothing broken or disturbed the next day so we must conclude that the crime could only have been carried out with inside help. The only males that live here are yourself and your eldest son. All your house staff are female. Therefore it stands to reason that if there was inside help it would almost certainly be a woman.

ROUGH *looks at* **DREW**.

You seem to have gone pale, sir. Are you all right?

DREW *straightens himself.*

DREW. Perfectly... thank you.

ROUGH. It must be the light then.

DREW *shakes his head.*

Have you never had anything make you go pale?

DREW. What are you talking about?

ROUGH. I am talking indirectly about a human body, sir, a little boy's human body, a little boy's body, which is somewhere, while we talk, on this earth. A little body alive or dead. A little body which is either crying for its mother, at this moment, in some dark place, or is lying mangled and strangled or with its throat cut under a hedge or at the bottom of a well. If the first is the case, if the baby is still alive then it is crying to you now, crying to its father.

He gets up.

Listen, how quiet it is, can't you hear it crying? And if the second is the case, sir, it is crying all the more. It is screaming and yelling for vengeance, sir, screaming and yelling for justice to the ends of the earth. Justice from its father and from its mother, and justice from society too, which I represent.

He puts down his drink on the mantel shelf and speaks angrily.

That is what we are talking about, sir. I don't think you quite understand.

DREW. My son is dead, sir. The case is closed. Have you any fresh evidence? If so, tell me what it is.

He stares at **ROUGH**.

Who are you, Inspector, and why have you come here?

ROUGH. Mr Drew, it has been six months since your son disappeared and I have a feeling, an impression...

DREW. I asked if you had any fresh evidence. A feeling is not evidence, I fancy.

ROUGH. No, sir. But a feeling is sometimes a good deal better than evidence. It was because of a feeling I had recently that a middle aged sailor, a very formidable middle aged sailor, Mr Drew, swung from a rope at Norwich just two days ago. And now I have a feeling here,

DREW. What sort of feeling?

ROUGH. You have a daughter, I remember.

DREW. Yes, Ellen.

ROUGH. Has she gone to bed?

DREW. Yes.

ROUGH. My notes from the original investigation imply that she had a feeling of sorts, that she thought she knew something. Is that so?

DREW. She dreams a great deal and walks in her sleep. There's nothing to be got out of her.

ROUGH. Ah... we mustn't turn away the dreamers. It's the dreamers who have the feelings, you know. I should like to speak to your daughter again, and find out what her feelings are.

DREW. Unfortunately she's in bed.

ROUGH. Yes. You told me so.

He stands up and places his empty glass on the drinks table.

DREW. Never mind about my daughter's feelings. I'm much more interested in yours. What sort of feelings have you?

ROUGH. About people in this house, Mr Drew. About two people in particular.

DREW. Which two people?

ROUGH. Yourself for one.

DREW. Myself?

ROUGH. Yes.

DREW. And who else?

ROUGH. Your governess, Miss Fry. Or rather the pair of you together.

DREW. Why should we be taken together?

ROUGH. I don't know. Unless you were taken with Miss Fry. Are you taken with her, Mr Drew?

DREW. Are you suggesting that I'm carrying on an illicit affair with a governess in my employ?

ROUGH. It's been known, Mr Drew. It's been known. Are you carrying on an illicit affair with a governess in your employ?

DREW. What has this to do with my child?

ROUGH. That's what I want to know. Mr Drew, I have a strong feeling that no one came from the outside and took your baby. Someone from inside went out. What is Miss Fry to you, Mr Drew?

ROUGH *has risen and they stand facing each other.*

DREW. Will you leave Miss Fry out of this.

ROUGH. Come now. I'm going to question her in a moment. What is she to you, Mr Drew?

DREW *just stares at him.*

Why does the mention of Miss Fry so upset you, sir?

He waits for **DREW** *to reply.*

What secret is there between you? Why do you oppose me so vehemently?

DREW. You shall not bring Miss Fry into this. Do you hear?

ROUGH. I should not have to go far to do that.

DREW. What do you mean?

ROUGH. She's listening just outside, sir. She is waiting and listening, just outside.

DREW *is totally indignant at this suggestion.*

DREW. Miss Fry is not the sort that listens.

ROUGH. All the same, sir. She is outside, trying to listen.

DREW. Where?

ROUGH. You have a great admiration for her character, haven't you, sir?

DREW. Miss Fry would not listen.

ROUGH. You love her, don't you. You have loved her for some time.

DREW *is deeply thrown by these accusations.*

I have a suspicion that you are not a wicked man. But I believe there is something more about Miss Fry than you know. I believe there is more about all this than any of us perhaps knows.

DREW. Miss Fry wouldn't listen.

ROUGH. Go and see, sir. Go on,

DREW *goes towards the door.*

Not the door. The window.

DREW *hesitates, then opens the French windows and peers out into the darkness.*

DREW. Miss Fry, Miss Fry... Are you there, Miss Fry?

MISS FRY. *(V.O.)* Do you want me, sir?

DREW. Come in, Miss Fry. Come in.

MISS FRY, *wearing a shawl, enters.*

What were you doing in the garden, my dear?

MISS FRY. Walking. Walking in the wind to clear my head. I love to walk in the wind, don't you?

DREW. Yes, I suppose so. I don't quite follow though, were you...

MISS FRY. Don't you, Mr Rogers? Don't you love to walk in the wind?

ROUGH. You're a romantic, Miss Fry. I can see that. Catching the effect of the night, eh? But you'd better close the window and come in or you'll catch cold. You look frozen to me. Come to the fire.

MISS FRY. No. I'm not cold. I'm quite warm. Aren't you two men still talking business?

ROUGH. No. We've finished. At least I think we have, haven't we?

DREW. Yes.

MISS FRY. What were you talking about?

ROUGH. We weren't talking about anything very nice.

MISS FRY. Oh I see. I know what that means.

ROUGH. What's that, Miss Fry?

MISS FRY. You were talking about our loss, weren't you? It is always with us. But then I think it will always be.

ROUGH. Yes. Unless he was found alive.

MISS FRY. How do you mean?

ROUGH. The loss... it wouldn't be there any more, would it?

MISS FRY. No. Then it wouldn't.

ROUGH. What's your view of this business, Miss Fry?

MISS FRY. In what way?

ROUGH. You don't think he's alive, do you?

MISS FRY. What makes you think that?

He shakes his head.

ROUGH. Just your tone. Do you think it was revenge?

MISS FRY. It might be. But who should want revenge?

ROUGH. Who indeed?

MISS FRY. I don't think it's my place to say, sir, but if you press me to answer I would say that I think that he is dead, murdered, and I don't think his remains will ever be found.

ROUGH *studies her.*

ROUGH. And that's what you think has happened?

DREW. Miss Fry...

MISS FRY. Yes.

DREW. This gentleman's name isn't Rogers.

MISS FRY *smiles a small secret smile.*

MISS FRY. I never imagined it was.

DREW. His real name is Rough, and he's a police detective. You don't have to answer him unless you want to.

ROUGH. You needn't have said that.

DREW. You needn't have come to my house, Inspector.

She laughs.

MISS FRY. Oh, how absurd! How absurd you men are. Do you think I didn't know? Do you think I didn't guess?

She shakes **ROUGH** *'s hand.*

How do you do, Inspector.

ROUGH. How do you do.

MISS FRY. I'm more than delighted to meet you. Have you any news?

KATE *enters and curtsies.*

KATE. Excuse me, sir.

DREW. Yes.

KATE. There's a gentleman below to see the gentleman up here, sir.

ROUGH. Thank you, Kate.

He takes out his watch and studies it carefully.

Excuse me,

He goes.

KATE. Am I to bring in the tea, sir?

DREW. Yes... yes Kate.

KATE. With an extra cup, sir?

DREW. Yes, Kate, with an extra cup.

KATE. Thank you, sir.

She leaves.

MISS FRY. How silly you are. Why didn't you tell me.

DREW. I don't know, really. I'm sorry.

MISS FRY. So you should be. Mr Rogers, indeed!

DREW. Why were you listening outside?

MISS FRY. What do you mean?

DREW. Weren't you listening?

MISS FRY. I was taking a walk? Can't I take a walk in the garden if I wish?

DREW. Of course. I'm sorry... I'm sorry.

He attempts to put his arm around her waist.

I knew you couldn't be listening.

MISS FRY *replies coldly.*

MISS FRY. Let go of me, please, sir. I listen? Is that what you think?

DREW. No, I knew you wouldn't.

He lets go of her.

I'm sorry. I've said I'm sorry. I love you.

MISS FRY. Then it seems you love an eavesdropper.

DREW. I'm sorry.

MISS FRY. Then don't say such things ever again.

She kisses his cheek.

If he has nothing new to say why is he here.

DREW *shakes his head.*

DREW. I don't know. He won't leave, and I can't seem to get rid of him.

MISS FRY. I've never heard you admit that before.

DREW. Do you want rid of him?

MISS FRY. Yes. I'd like him to go.

DREW. Very well.

He sits down.

I miss my son more than anything in the world, and I want him back. If this man has come to help us I for one am only too willing to offer my assistance.

MISS FRY. What are you talking about?

DREW *shakes his head.*

DREW. I'm sorry. It just occurred to me you might know something. Something you were keeping back, perhaps for my sake. I know I've never shown it before but I love my son and I want him back if it is at all possible. I want him back very badly indeed.

MISS FRY. Don't you think I do, too?

DREW. I'm sorry, I know you do. The man's upset me.

ROUGH *enters.*

ROUGH. Ah, here we are again. Sorry about that. A man of mine, sir, on an errand. All the way from Camberwell.

MISS FRY. From Camberwell!

ROUGH. Yes... perhaps you know the area?

She shakes her head.

DREW. How did he get here at this time of night?

ROUGH. He took a cab, or rather he allowed a cab to take him, to be more accurate. It'd take a strong man to haul a cab all that way, wouldn't it?

He smiles.

DREW. Inspector Rough, my family and I are about to have tea before we go to bed. If I furnish a cab, will you allow it to take you out of this neighbourhood.

ROUGH *stares at him.*

MISS FRY. Oh, no. We can't be so rude as to turn the Inspector away like that. Mr Drew please ask him to stay.

DREW *is dumbfounded by this turnaround.*

DREW. But Miss Fry...

MISS FRY. Sit down Inspector, please. Have you any fresh news? You must have or you wouldn't have come. Please sit down.

ROUGH. No, Miss Fry, I'm afraid I've nothing fresh.

MISS FRY. How disappointing. Then why have you come? To question us? You must have questioned Mr Drew. Don't you want to question me? Heaven knows we were questioned enough at the time, but we shan't mind a few questions more.

She sits down on the settee.

ROUGH. You seem very anxious to be questioned, Miss Fry.

MISS FRY. Naturally. The frustration of not knowing what happened causes great anxiety.

ROUGH. Is that because you're certain that nothing will come to light?

MISS FRY. To light?

She frowns at the inspector.

I don't understand, Inspector.

DREW. How dare you speak to Miss Fry like that. If you have any questions...

DREW *is unaware that he has raised his voice.*

ROUGH. Never mind about...

MISS FRY. Shh... shh... shh. Quiet. Quiet, please gentlemen.

The door opens and **ROBERT** *appears in the doorway, carrying the tea tray. He is gently inebriated.* **MRS DREW** *follows him into the room.*

MRS DREW. Robert, please be careful with the china darling. Please be careful.

He skids to a halt in front of his father.

ROBERT. Good evening, father. Your Mother says I'm tipsy I mean my mother says you're tipsy. I mean I'm tipsy. Do I appear to be tipsy?

DREW *rather welcomes this distraction.*

DREW. Don't stand there talking nonsense, Bob. Put the tea things on the desk. Let's all have tea.

MRS DREW. I'll deal with it, darling.

ROBERT. I'm all right about the legs. I'm just a bit hazy about the top.

DREW. You're a bit hazy about the top permanently. Go and sit down.

DREW *introduces the inspector.*

This is Detective Inspector Rough, Winifred. My wife.

MRS DREW. Oh, how do you do, Inspector?

ROUGH. How do you do?

MRS DREW. Do you take cream and sugar?

ROUGH. Both if I may.

ROBERT. Excuse me, sir. Are you an explorer?

ROUGH. No sir. Do I look like one?

ROBERT. You don't exactly look like one. I asked if you were one.

ROUGH. No, I'm not.

ROBERT. Why not?

ROUGH. It never took me that way, that's all, young man.

He takes the tea offered to him.

Thank you, Mrs Drew.

ROBERT. I've been down to the House of Commons.

DREW. Oh, how did you get in there?

ROBERT. I have friends. It's all a lot of damned nonsense as far as I can see.

DREW. Yes. You've got something there.

He frowns at his son.

But there's no need to swear.

ROBERT. What we want is a man like Cromwell. If Cromwell were alive today he'd take a stand about it, wouldn't he, sir?

ROUGH. Well, actually, if Cromwell were alive today he would be rather too old to take a stand about anything. But I see your point, young man.

MISS FRY *takes her tea and goes back to her chair.* **DREW** *hands his son a cup of tea.*

DREW. Drink your tea, Bob. Drink your tea.

MRS DREW. Why are you here, Inspector. Is there anything new?

ROUGH. No, ma'am. Nothing I'm afraid. Just going over some details with your husband. Nothing to worry you...

He suddenly stops, goes to the door and opens it. **ELLEN** *walks into the room. She appears and responds perfectly normally but it soon becomes clear that she is in fact sleep walking.* **KATE** *stands anxiously behind her in the doorway.*

ELLEN. Bouillir... *Je bous, nous bouillons... Je bous, nous bouillons... Je bous, nous bouillons.* Yes, Miss Fry, I remember. I remember about baby.

MRS DREW *immediately recognises the state her daughter is in.*

MRS DREW. We must guide her back.

MISS FRY. Yes, we must.

MISS FRY *moves towards* **ELLEN** *but is restrained by* **ROUGH**.

ROUGH. No, don't, Miss Fry.

ELLEN. I remember, I remember, The house where I was born, I remember, I remember...

She struggles to remember.

Sitting on the lawn... No, that's wrong. I remember Miss Fry. I remember all about baby. I remember, I remember.

MISS FRY. Let me help her.

ROUGH. Miss Fry... let her be. Let her talk.

ELLEN *moves closer to the oil lamp on the table, and stares into it.*

It's bright. How bright it is. The sun's come up, baby. The sun's come up. Come to the window. We'll go out and play.

She shades her face from the glare.

No, it's not the sun, baby. It's the lamp. We must put the lamp out.

ELLEN *attempts to trim the lamp.*

Out goes the lamp, and we go to bed. Where is it, baby? Where is it? Where is the lamp?

ROUGH *gently dims the lamp.*

It's getting dark and we must go to bed. Where are you? It's dark. Baby, where have you gone? Where are you?

ELLEN *looks round the room, searching for baby.*

Baby, where are you? Are you hiding, you naughty child? All right. I'll find you.

She starts to move around the room.

MRS DREW. Oughtn't we to guide her to bed?

ROUGH. Let her be.

DREW. What's there to gain by this?

ROUGH. Quiet...

MISS FRY. We must help her.

ELLEN. Miss Fry? Is that you, Miss Fry? I've lost baby. Miss Fry I've lost baby.

She moves a few paces.

Oh, I'm sorry, Miss Fry. I'm being a chatterbox again. I'll remember. I'll remember. *J'ai recontre le monsieur dont vous m'avez parle.*

ROUGH *takes* **MISS FRY***'s shawl and puts it gently around* **ELLEN***'s shoulder's.*

I have met the gentleman who spoke to me. No, that's wrong, Miss Fry. I'll remember. I'll remember.

ELLEN*'s voice changes as she becomes more and more excited.*

If you pinch me, I shall tell father. My arm is black and blue.

Her voice is strangled with pain.

Oh, Miss Fry, don't... don't.

She moves very close to **MISS FRY**.

You are not to pinch me. Don't... don't.

MISS FRY *backs away.*

I'll remember. I'll remember. As long as you don't pinch me. I'll remember,

All the papers spill onto the floor. **ELLEN** *picks up an ink bottle.*

Your scent, Miss Fry. Your scent. Now I remember. Your scent, Miss Fry.

ROUGH *takes the ink bottle from her.*

I went into your room. That's it. But something's the matter. Am I asleep or am I dreaming? Do you know what happens to those who dream too much. They are pinched awake. Shall I pinch myself awake.

ELLEN *tries to pinch her own arm. She begins to whimper.* **ROUGH** *gently restrains her, speaking soothingly.*

ROUGH. Don't pinch yourself, my dear. Sit down. Sit down.

He sits her down.

ELLEN. Who is that? Is that my father?

ROUGH. Yes.

ELLEN. Miss Fry pinches me, father. She pinches me black and blue.

ROUGH. The scent... what do you remember? You went into Miss Fry's room the night baby was taken?

ELLEN. *J'ai rencontre le monsieur dont vous m'avez parle...*

ROUGH. You went into Miss Fry's room?

ELLEN. Yes.

ROUGH. The night baby was taken.

ELLEN. Yes. The night baby was taken. I know I went in because when I woke up I could smell your scent. But if I was in your room why didn't you stop me? Because you weren't there. I saw you in the nursery. You took baby, Miss Fry. You thought I was asleep, and so I was. I was half asleep, but I saw you. I saw you come in, bend over baby's cot and take baby out. The black cloak, Miss Fry your black ugly cloak. I remember. Why did you take baby? What have you done to him? Have you killed him? He's ours, not yours. Give him back, Miss Fry... give him back.

Before anyone can stop her **MISS FRY** *grabs* **ELLEN**, *shakes her violently, and slaps her across the face.*

MISS FRY. Wake up... wake up!

She slaps her again.

Wake up.

ELLEN *screams.*

ELLEN. Aagh... aagh...

MRS DREW *is shocked by* **MISS FRY**'*s brutality.*

ROBERT. Stop that. Stop it.

MISS FRY. She has to be woken up.

She cradles **ELLEN** *in her arms.*

It's all right, Ellen. It's me. It's all right, it's all right.

MRS DREW. How could you do that?

MISS FRY. When she's hysterical she has to be slapped. There, Ellen, it's all right...

ELLEN *quietens.*

MRS DREW. Why did you strike her? Why?

ELLEN *begins to realise where she is.*

ELLEN. Where am I? Where am I?

MISS FRY. It's alright my darling.

ROBERT. You've been sleep walking, that's all.

ELLEN. I was dreaming about baby. Where's baby?

ROBERT. We don't know.

ELLEN *runs from the room folowed by* **MRS DREW** *and* **ROBERT**. **KATE** *closes the door after them.*

DREW. Why did you strike her, Miss Fry?

MISS FRY. She was in danger.

ROUGH *takes control of the situation.*

ROUGH. There now. We needn't go on about it. Your daughter doesn't seem to have taken harm.

MISS FRY. It was for her own good.

KATE *helps* **ROBERT** *and* **MRS DREW** *to take* **ELLEN** *to her bedroom.*

ROUGH. Sit down, Miss Fry. The child's upset you, I'm afraid. Shall I pour you another cup?

MISS FRY. Yes. Please do.

ROUGH. I'm afraid it'll be rather cold.

He smiles affably at **MISS FRY**.

Dear me, how she rambled on. She thought the lamp was the sun. Did you see that Drew? She thought the lamp was the sun.

ROUGH *pours the tea.*

I thought she was going to burn herself. Then she thought it was dark, and that she'd lost baby. Then she thought she was at her lessons with you. You seem to have made a strong impression on that girl's mind.

He hands a cup to **MISS FRY**.

MISS FRY. Thank you Inspector.

ROUGH. *J'ai rencontre le monsieur dont vous m'avez parle.* I have met the gentleman of whom you spoke to me.

He shakes his head.

A difficult sentence, especially for a sleep walking little girl. And then all that business about the pinching. She seemed quite frightened. You wouldn't pinch a little girl, because she was bad at her lessons, would you, Miss Fry?

MISS FRY. Do I look as though I would?

ROUGH. No, I can't say you do.

DREW *is looking extremely disquieted.*

All the same she thought she'd been pinched. She said her arm was black and blue. She probably pinches herself in her sleep. In fact she tried to pinch herself awake, didn't she?

DREW. Inspector, couldn't we deal with all this perhaps another time. What has just happened is very upsetting and if I may say so it's mostly your doing.

ROUGH. Why do say that?

DREW. If you'd let the child be guided back to bed, none of this would have occured.

ROUGH. I thought perhaps she might know something. She kept saying she did, didn't she? Of course the ramblings of a sleep walking child would not be permissible in court. Yes... I suppose I did wrong. Yet there might be something there. She might have seen something while she was asleep.

MISS FRY. How do you mean? If she was asleep how could she have seen anything?

ROUGH. Yes. That's what so strange. She covered that point, didn't you notice? She said "You thought I was asleep, Miss Fry, and so I was. I was half asleep, but I saw you." Didn't you hear that?

MISS FRY. No.

ROUGH. Didn't you, Mr Drew?

DREW *shakes his head.*

"You thought I was asleep, Miss Fry, but I saw you. You took baby, Miss Fry. You took baby. I saw you, Miss Fry, I saw you."

DREW. Inspector, are you accusing Miss Fry of somehow being involved?

ROUGH. My dear sir, not in the least. I just thought the child might have really seen something that night, that's all. She might have been half awake, half asleep as she said she was, and have seen something, that's all. I'm sure you don't mind, Miss Fry do you?

MISS FRY. No. Not in the least.

ROUGH *turns sharply on* **DREW**.

ROUGH. All I am trying to do is get at the truth.

He turns to **MISS FRY**

Then, there was the business about your scent bottle. From what she said she walked into your room that night, and used your scent, because she was covered with it the next morning. And if you'd been there you would have stopped her. All senseless dreams, I suppose?

MISS FRY. Yes. No one touched the scent bottle.

ROUGH. And yet she said she smelt of it the next morning when she awoke. You're certain you were in your room all that night?

MISS FRY. Naturally. Where else should I have been?

ROUGH. Indeed. Where else?

He glances at **DREW**.

I was particularly struck by her reference to the cloak.

MISS FRY. Oh, what was that?

ROUGH. Don't you remember. In your black cloak, Miss Fry. Bending over the cot in your ugly black cloak. Have you got a black cloak, Miss Fry?

MISS FRY. Not that I know of.

ROUGH. No. I'm sure you haven't. You're much too charming to wear such things. You've never seen her in black clothes have you, Mr Drew?

DREW *shakes his head.*

DREW. No, I haven't.

He turns back to **MISS FRY**.

ROUGH. Yet that's what she said, didn't she? Where did she get the idea? I suppose you haven't got a black cloak, Miss Fry. One you've hardly ever worn, hidden away? Something you've never worn except perhaps for that one night.

MISS FRY. What do you mean except perhaps for that one night?

ROUGH. Nothing, Miss Fry. Nothing at all.

MISS FRY. I've told you, I've no such cloak.

ROUGH. But she must have got the idea from somewhere. Haven't you got anything like it? Come to think of it we could easily find out...

MISS FRY. How?

ROUGH. Why, we could go upstairs now, if you like and see. What about that? Shall we go and look?

He smiles affably and stands up.

MISS FRY. I have no such item.

ROUGH. No, Miss Fry. I know. But shall we go and see if we can find something that could be mistaken for a cloak.

MISS FRY. There's no need.

ROUGH. Don't take on so. We're only talking about dreams, aren't we?

He shakes his head.

Unfortunately she couldn't tell us anymore, could she, because at that moment you woke her up. You shook her and slapped her across the face.

He frowns.

Why did you do that, Miss Fry?

There is a knock at the door.

You said you hit her to control her. For her own good. Are you sure that's why? Are you sure you didn't hit her because you knew you were done for? And done for you are, Miss Fry, believe me.

KATE *enters and curtsies.*

KATE. Excuse me sir.

She addresses **ROUGH.**

There is a gentleman downstairs sir. Says he needs to have a word.

ROUGH. Thank you Kate.

He follows **KATE** *out, glancing back at* **MISS FRY**, *before closing the door behind him.*

MISS FRY. How dare he. Didn't you say you'd throw him out?

DREW *seems stunned by events.*

DREW. What's all this about a black cloak?

MISS FRY. Do you suspect me now? Do you suspect me?

He doesn't reply, he just stares at her.

Then I shall leave. If you'll not protect me, I shall leave.

She makes for the door.

DREW. Come back. In the name of God come back.

He goes to her and holds her.

MISS FRY. I've been grossly insulted. If you will not protect me then I shall go. Then where will you find your kisses?

She breaks away.

Where will you find your kisses then?

DREW. For God's sake keep calm. The man's a maniac. I'll send him away.

MISS FRY. He's trying to catch me out. There's no such cloak upstairs.

DREW. Do you think I don't trust you?

MISS FRY. Look me in the eyes and say you believe me.

DREW. I believe you, my darling.

MISS FRY. There's no cloak I tell you.

DREW. I know there's not. I know. The whole thing's mad. The man's a maniac. He shan't insult you any more. I shall send him away.

MISS FRY. Listen. Go and get the cloak.

DREW. What?

MISS FRY. Go and get it.

DREW. What do you mean?

MISS FRY. Go and get it. It's at the bottom of my wardrobe at the back. You trust me, don't you? He's trying to catch me out, that's all. You trust me don't you?

DREW. Yes.

MISS FRY. Then go and get the cloak and hide it. Trust me. He's trying to catch me out.

She grabs hold of him.

You do trust me?

DREW. Yes... Yes, I'll do what you say.

He goes towards the door.

He shan't question you any more. I'll kick the brute out.

MISS FRY. He's setting me off. He's setting me off.

Before **DREW** *can leave,* **ROUGH** *enters.*

DREW. You take wonderful liberties with my house, don't you, sir?

ROUGH. I suppose I do. But then wonderful things have been going on in your house just recently, believe me.

DREW. Inspector... you can go back to your damned police station, or wherever you come from, If you have any questions to put to me or to members of my household you can do so at the proper time and at the proper place. Do you understand?

ROUGH. Of course, sir.

DREW *scoffs.*

DREW. After all you admitted you have no new evidence.

ROUGH. Not exactly evidence. I just need to ask your governess a few questions, that is all.

DREW. Miss Fry is not going to say another word tonight.

ROUGH. I see.

He picks up his coat and hat, as if to leave. In the face of this seeming retreat **DREW** *cannot resist the temptation to bully.*

DREW. I don't believe you're a real policeman are you?

ROUGH *puts his hat and coat down again.*

Show me your credentials? Go on man, show me them.

ROUGH *slowly turns to face him.*

ROUGH. I can assure you sir that I have plenty of credentials. But more importantly I have a witness.

DREW. What witness?

ROUGH. Someone you know full well. Someone you sacked six months ago, the day your child went missing.

ROUGH *opens the door, and calls down the corridor.*

Johnson!!

RUSH, *handcuffed to* **JOHNSON**, *a detective, and accompanied by a female detective, carrying a black cloak, appear in the doorway.* **MISS FRY** *gasps.*

DREW. What's this man doing here?

RUSH *addresses* **DREW**

RUSH. Good evening Guv'nor. Pleased to see you again.

MISS FRY *stares at him.*

Why, my dear! My precious darlin! It looks as though it's all up don't it, old girl.

She backs away)

'Ere... don't pretend you don't recognise me? Don't wound my feelings, darlin.

MISS FRY *turns to* **DREW**.

MISS FRY. See what they are doing. They are trying to set me off. Send them away.

DREW. This is preposterous...

RUSH. It's all up with us, I'm afraid, old girl. I've gone and turned the old Queen's evidence. The dear, lovely, old Queen. I'd know me if I were you.

MISS FRY *appeals to* **DREW**.

MISS FRY. Don't let them set me off, please.

RUSH *laughs*

RUSH. Don't take on so. I've told them everything. I had to, my dear.

RUSH *tries to step nearer but is restrained by the detective.*

MISS FRY. He's mad. He's...

MISS FRY *claps her hands to her ears.*

Take him away. Take him away.

DREW *stands there totally shocked by events.*

Can't you see what they are doing. Can't you see it's a plot...

ROUGH *steps closer to her.*

Can't you see he's trying to set me off. Send them away, please. Don't let them set me off, please.

ROUGH *starts to chant a curious and hypnotic refrain.*

ROUGH. I am the Rose... I am the Rose... I am the Rose.

MISS FRY *struggles to avoid him. She turns desperately to* **DREW**.

MISS FRY. Don't let him... please... please... please.

ROUGH. I am the Rose... I am the Rose... I am the Rose.

She attempts to block out **ROUGH** *by reciting the alphabet, faster and ever faster.*

MISS FRY. A, b, c, d, e, f, g. A, b, c, d, e, f, g. A, b, c, d, e, f, g.

She screams.

Don't let him set me off.

ROUGH. I am the Rose... I am the Rose... I am the Rose...

ROUGH*'s gaze is hypnotic.*

MISS FRY. A, b, c, d, e, f, g. A, b, c, d, e, f, g...

ROUGH. I am the Rose of what? I am the Rose of what...?

MISS FRY. A, b, c, d, e, f, g.

ROUGH. I am the Rose of what? I am the Rose of what...?

She starts to quote from the Song of Solomon.

MISS FRY. I am the Rose of Sharon, and the Lily of the Valleys...

ROUGH *prompts her.*

ROUGH. As the lily among thorns. As the lily among thorns.

MISS FRY. As the lily among thorns. I am the Rose of Sharon, and the lily of the valleys. As a lily among thorns, so is my love among the daughters.

She is transfixed by **ROUGH** *'s eyes.*

Oh my love, let me hear thy voice, for sweet is thy voice, and thy countenance is comely.

ROUGH. The banqueting house. The banqueting house.

Her voice becomes rapturous.

MISS FRY. He brought me to the banqueting house, and his banner over me was love. Stay me with flagons, comfort me with apples, for I am sick of love. For you the winter is past, the rain is over and gone...

She speaks with yearning ecstasy.

Oh my love, let me hear thy voice, for sweet is thy voice, and thy countenance is comely.

She moves towards **ROUGH**.

By night on my bed I sought him whom my soul loveth. I sought him, but I found him not.

DREW. Stop her... please. Stop her.

MISS FRY. I will rise now, and go about the city. In the streets and in the broad ways I will seek him whom my soul loveth. Behold, thou art fair, my love. Thy lips are like a thread of scarlet, and thy speech is comely. Thy temples are like a piece of pomegranate within thy locks.

DREW. Oh, my God!

She clasps her hands together in prayer.

MISS FRY. Let him kiss me with the kisses of his mouth, for thy love is better than wine. Let him kiss me with the kisses of...

She lapses into a quiet submissive world. **ROUGH** *sits her gently on the settee, and speaks to her soothingly.*

ROUGH. Listen to me carefully Miss Fry. Just listen carefully. Was your name formally Lomas?

MISS FRY. Sarah Lomas.

ROUGH. Where were you brought up?

MISS FRY. In Cheltenham.

ROUGH. But you didn't go to school there?

MISS FRY. No... I was sent to a private school in Gloucester.

ROUGH. While you were there did you run away with the headmistress's baby boy?

MISS FRY, *with a hunted look, just stares at him.*

Did you take the baby?

She nods

MISS FRY. Yes.

ROUGH. What happened then?

MISS FRY. I was arrested.

ROUGH. Where?

MISS FRY. In Bristol... we were going to America.

DREW. No... no.

ROUGH *indicates* **DREW** *to be quiet.*

ROUGH. You were sent to prison.

MISS FRY *nods.*

MISS FRY. They took my baby from me.

ROUGH. When you were released you took up a position as governess with a family in Northumberland. It was there you met Mr Rush?

MISS FRY. Yes.

ROUGH. Where there was also a baby boy.

MISS FRY. My baby.

ROUGH. You and Rush stole the baby and took it to London with you?

RUSH. It was nothing to do with me.

ROUGH. Why did you run away?

MISS FRY. They were trying to take my baby.

ROUGH. What happened then?

MISS FRY. They wouldn't let me keep baby.

ROUGH. You and Rush both received long prison sentences. When you came out the two of you took a place together in Camberwell.

MISS FRY. Yes.

ROUGH. And changed your name to Fry...

MISS FRY *starts to moan.*

... and then with false references came to work here as Governess.

She covers her head with her arms and curls up on the settee.

Miss Fry... did you in the middle of the night, with the help of Rush, take the baby from this house?

MISS FRY. Yes... we took him home.

ROUGH *takes the black cloak from the female detective and shows it to* **MISS FRY**.

ROUGH. Is this the cloak, which we found upstairs, the one you wore that night?

MISS FRY *nods and* **ROUGH** *hands the cloak back.*

RUSH. I never helped her. She just turned up at the place with the baby. What was I to do?

ROUGH. Johnson. Take him out.

The detective takes **RUSH** *out.*

You took your baby back to Camberwell.

MISS FRY. Yes... yes.

ROUGH. But you continued to live here? So who looks after the child?

MISS FRY. A neighbour.

MISS FRY *cries out.*

He's mine, he's my baby. He's mine.

She curls up in a ball on the settee.

DREW. Where is my child now? Is he... safe?

ROUGH. Your wife is with him. Upstairs to the nursery.

DREW *looks across at the inert body of* **MISS FRY**.

DREW. I... loved her. When you came here this evening you already knew.

ROUGH *nods.*

ROUGH. Mostly. We interrogated Rush and in order to save his skin, he was only too willing to co-operate.

DREW *shakes his head.*

I'm afraid I've played false with you, Mr Drew, but I had to be quite certain that no one else was involved.

DREW. Why... why did she do it?

ROUGH *shrugs.*

ROUGH. I've come to understand the way criminals behave and I also understand to a degree how maniacs behave. In the eyes of the law they are one and the same. Only their motives differ. Why Miss Fry takes these children we shall probably never fully understand.

*(***ROUGH** *looks at the inert form of* **MISS FRY** *on the settee.)*

I believe her motive is power.

DREW. Power?

ROUGH. Yes, sir. Power.

There is a long silence.

DREW. She mustn't suffer. She mustn't be put away.

ROUGH. She must be put away, sir, but she needn't suffer. You have the money, and she need not suffer.

At that moment the door opens and **MRS DREW** *enters.*

MRS DREW. George... George... baby's come back! They've brought back my baby...

MISS FRY *calmly gets up and embraces* **MRS DREW**.

MISS FRY. You are mistaken, my dear. He is my baby.

MRS DREW *steps back aghast.* **MISS FRY** *speaks to her in a kindly tone.*

After all you are ugly. I am beautiful and the man is mine? And if he is mine, so is his child.

ROUGH *steps forward to constrain her.*

The man is mine, ugly one, the man and his kisses. I am lovely. You mustn't think the baby yours.

MRS DREW *screams.*

MRS DREW. What are you saying?

MISS FRY. The baby is mine. The baby is mine.

ROUGH *nods towards the female detective,* **MISS WATSON**, *who steps forward. He speaks gently to* **MISS FRY**.

ROUGH. Miss Fry, there are a lot of people in this room, are there not.

MISS FRY. The room is thick with them.

ROUGH. Better to go outside. These people have got designs on your baby, and you don't want to stay on those terms, do you? Here's Miss Watson. Why don't you go with her? You can talk about your baby with her.

MISS FRY *looks round the room, picks up her bag and starts to rummage in it.*

MISS FRY. They say I paint. They say I am so lovely because I paint. Do you think I paint, Inspector? Because I do. That is why I am so lovely.

She opens the pot of rouge.

Shall I paint you? Shall I paint you?

ROUGH *stands immobile as she methodically puts two streaks of rouge across his face.*

There now, you are painted, you beautiful man...

She turns to **MISS WATSON**.

My dear, delighted to meet you! Shall we go? I've really no desire to stay here. Come, let us go.

She goes to the door.

How nice to meet a woman. We shall have a woman's chat about womanly things shan't we. Do you know I always hated men.

She turns back and slowly regards **DREW** *and* **ROUGH**.

I've always hated men.

MISS FRY *and the female detective leave.*

MRS DREW. I don't understand... I don't understand.

ROUGH. It was Miss Fry who took your baby.

MRS DREW. *stands open mouthed in disbelief.* **DREW** *comforts his wife.*

Early this morning I had to attend a poor devil who succeeded in killing his wife and child, but had no such luck with himself. At noon I interviewed a young man who had stolen some money and was white with fear and remorse, while his mother and father stood ruined beside him. This evening I came here and brought another sort of ruin. The world's full of ruin, and full of poor devils. But it's full of building too, and it's full of pity. We must cultivate pity.

He picks up his overcoat.

Good night.

He leaves. **DREW** *and his wife stand there in silence. Slowly tears start to run down* **DREW***'s face. He is choking with emotion and in a still small voice he utters.*

MRS DREW. She'll be all right.

DREW. Poor deluded devils. All of us.

The End

Lightning Source UK Ltd.
Milton Keynes UK
UKHW011154120619
344251UK00006B/705/P